ZOODIKERS: A BESTIARY

ZOODIKERS: A BESTIARY

POEMS

FLOWER CONROY

UNIVERSITY OF TAMPA PRESS

Copyright © 2025 by Flower Conroy. All rights reserved.

Manufactured in the United States of America
Printed on acid-free paper ∞
First Edition

On the Cover: *Fauna*, Colin and Kristine Poole, fired clay, 38 x 29 x 20 in. Private collection, courtesy of the artists. www.colinpoole.com. www.kristinepoole.com. Fauna is a goddess from Roman mythology most frequently seen as the wife and/or sister of the more familiar Faunus (Pan in Greek mythology). Fauna, according to some sources, is seen as a goddess of the woodlands, a representation of the wild sexuality of women, and an expression of fertility and the life force.

Cover design by Jay Aja

No part of this book may be reproduced, stored in a retrieval system, or transmitted in any form or by any means, electronic, mechanical, photocopying, recording, or otherwise, except as may be expressly permitted by the applicable copyright statutes or in writing by the publisher.

The University of Tampa Press
401 West Kennedy Boulevard
Tampa, FL 33606

ISBN (pbk.) 978-1-59732-220-1
ISBN (hbk.) 978-1-59732-221-8
ISBN (ebk.) 978-1-59732-222-5

Library of Congress Control Number:
2025933895

Browse & order online at
http://www.utampapress.org

For my family.

For my wife, V—who makes all this and more possible.

TABLE OF CONTENTS

Zymurgy • 1
Holy Fool • 2
Absinthe Makes the Heart Grow Flaunter • 3
Snail • 4
Echidna • 5
Dodo • 6
OUIJA • 7
Horseshoe Crab • 8
Tardigrade • 9
Bigfoot • 10
Wolf • 11
Bloodhound • 12
Rabbit • 13
6EQUJ5 • 14
Velvet • 15
Diamondback • 16
Parroting • 17
Incubus • 18
Gumby • 19
Coat of Arms • 20
Armadillo • 21
Platypus • 22
Turtle • 23
Quakers/Quackers • 24
Confession(al) • 25

Walrus • 26
Lazarus Taxa • 27
Yak • 28
Phoenix • 29
Quagga • 30
Venus (Infers) • 31
Elephant • 32
Nudibranchs • 33
Gräfenberg Spot • 34
Yet(i) • 35
Ichthyosaurus • 36
Lobotomy • 37
Fog • 38
Drone • 39
Jackal • 40
Frog • 41
Vulture • 42
Mushroom • 43
Ibex • 44
Onanism • 45
Kkaahkkaahrowch • 46
Lobster Shack • 47
Dearest • 48
Another Roadside Attraction • 49
Probably Bears • 50
Undertaker • 51
Maggot • 52
Sky Whale • 53
| {Pill[(ow) Talk]} Bug | • 54
Machine Deep Learning (Cento) • 55
Rhinoceros • 56

Nightmare • 57
Zero • 58
Flea • 59
Axolotl • 60
Fisher Cat • 61
Centipede • 62
Zwitterion • 63
Sestina • 64
Zonkey • 65

Notes • 66
Acknowledgements • 72
About the Author • 75
About the Book • 77

*When a species leaves the planet,
they take all of their sounds with them—
their heartbeat, their breath, their footfall,
their fluttering, their gallop, their cries,
their songs.*

CACONRAD

O conjureman, go on with us.

CAROL CONROY

Zymurgy

> *It is / A strange idea that one must say what*
> *one thinks in order to be understood*

So lemme get this *straight*—exactly how transparent must I be if I'm trying to get you to follow me into the burning city of body? Shall I get out the way my gayness, gouge my heart from its bonelocker & fasten it to kidskin glove, a blooded button? Confess I'm a vessel of dumbwonder whose heart's a panic room whose spine's ramshackled light; that I alienate into dreamstate, that I get off on mystery & quirk? Of course time's mirrorish. That still doesn't account for the chimney swift's dust bowl flight nor for what's uttered in restraint. If I seem fungal, oracular, sugary? Let me toast being an ecstasy chaser—I'm often lacking. When I realized my womb was a vat in which fermentation of life wouldn't ever happen? How deeplier inside. How nakedly before. But how undoubtedly dendrite thereafter. I'm sure I'd be aglow as a maraschino cherry were I gravid. Not that I've the stomach for being split through then dandy-stitched back up the middle; never mind gobsmacking terror of contracting, of keeping immaculate track—hours, mittens, milkbreath—that I can't even conceive how to mother

Holy Fool

Being in the middle of the ocean is like god; no matter where you look you can see into infinity. Something tricky & serene about it—pushing boundaries. A moment later my wife's snoring. Who is poor & who's rich here amidst the incessant flux? Shack of sun. Moon spackled motion. Even the dead feed. Unboiled bones the ripples. When were you last stranded? I mean truly. I mean utterly. I mean wholly holy alive beneath & alone? I've never fled for my life but I've begged for it. Of the greater delusions I—I also think hope I think time travel & forgiveness—of course implicit is redemption (& I swear I just witnessed a fish leap out & back into its sunken kingdom)—you've to understand like you I strove for *opus maximus*, to change myself by changing the world. And vice. Versa. In the short while I was gone the azalea've full forced their ultraviolet extravagance I'm sipping godsblood from mantra & soon the bayou's ancient reptiles will awake hungry & horny. A buttery sun's lacing the sudden greenery as it lowers. Some funny little spider's cleaning its fang & eye face just inches from my proxy. I wanted to be present atemporal but presence demands the moment at hand. If your habits will kill you are you suicidal? Coincidence I'm sure the nature of enlightenment & Fight Club share the same keep quiet motto, a feather falling nonverbal. **Praa**·fuht has two meanings—no witch yore chasing into the gorge us abyss, ignorance the bliss in blister

Absinthe Makes the
Heart Grow Flaunter

Nothing I say isn't going to not sound like me. Does mother fawns, to fawn is to fall for, burn is what the bark does but does stone eavesdrop hoarfrost? To extract any attar you must first decimate bloom. Elegiac lily's wake. Angel grip. It's not like I have tomatoes on my eyes, it's not as if I *wanted* to plunge leaning over bridge until hair flips leg dangling into the uncanny. It wasn't even a *what if* as much as it was a closering nearing couldn't embody. I hesitate to say *fata morgana* but pull might be reciprocal between worlds. As if emptiness were magnetized beckoning. Like the clairaudience of glass, a third ghostly tune in the syntax; I unfold as to know my own downfalling

Snail

Gill of night sails, lung of the garden; unlike my wrist you glide unfazed along guillotine blade gilding razor iridescent. Mica, soundmoon, organ veiled. You familiarize yourself with being alone; armored Sheela-na-gig shouldering helicline mansion calibrating increments of white noise pussyfooting a tightrope of your own pearly streaking. The way a tulip bends on the first spring Sunday counterclockwise to the light a hairsbreadth backwards in time to the beginning of ice. A cave, after all, is the sum dimension of its own slow-motion gutting. Thumbprint on the sensor panel which pricks my blood & reads it. Radii of 200 million years, whiff of tuberose, thin eye stems among collarbone & thistle. A few more centuries underwater & you are cupped in my hands. I need only to lift your coffin lid & edge inside to recover us. The side-effects of the fossil system are countless. A traveler divided. Unarticulated atmosphere, mull & shatter. Line by line right form is essential to any form. My footsteps echo steep before I step

Echidna

Blade rhumb lines the tongue—broadswords scorpion bonestone. I'm really sick but won't admit it. One by one the acupuncturist *tlcks* out the rostrum-like pins—forehead cheeks chin—save for the filiform splinter embedded in the meridian of my soft spot, crown of the governing vessel. Monster irresistible—like that satyred hippopotamus the rhino. Spiny spiky anteater. Hedgehog cousin. Half-woman half-squamate dwelling in an antler cave no outside world's iron age pierces. When I press the antenna hidden in my skull the mind's long lists of *past due & to do & will it so*. When I press harder: axis of a planet yet discovered, blood temples, glassblowing nerve hiss. Firmer still, a jet extirpates the sound barrier of retrograde amnesia, a bolt of frisson fernseeds dream into channels, salt of tinnitus slicks my throat. Crack & release, a drippy sensation along the spine, toe tingle. It's not the arrow skewering heart but—like a finger plugging the dam—or a cork in the socket—it's the pluckering out of that stopper—which kills you

Dodo

You've been thought rail, penguin, albatross, goose, vulture &or shrunken ostrich until finally designated ground pigeon. Accounts recording how easy your capture—*fearless* the sailors commented of your approaching. How grabbed by your foot & dangled you honked out & the others came scrambling. When you waddled your knot-arse right up to the pistol they in turn blamed you for your obsolescence. You'd think 13.8 billion years later we'd've gleaned a nugget of enlightenment, knowing the common denominator between a beluga & a shrew is a hair, that literally we're *One Human Family*, the helix traced back to a single cell. Hadn't Marie repeated *there is no us & them there is only us?* It would revert. If humanity perished before destroying it all nature would take over. Reclaim the labefaction. It's any apocalypse's nucleoplasm. And while it's getting harder to bear our collective grief among the accumulating horrors— we've still lavender & melody, we've still cosmic glitter & laughter but daily is (the) slaughter, people huddle or are, camps creep up in the thick hours & what happens within baffles (or should) the heart—I think it's fair to say some of us still've the god shattering rage to bash the gold gilded egg & lift each other up from the sharp mulch because if we don't—we'll all eschaton into the revelatory flames we'll all can of worms into the ether

OUIJA

I'm the bomb sniffing ideomotor revealing your known unknowns chaining floating letters; my bibliomaniac alphabet's misidentified internal forces'll demystify your human bafflement sieving the ashes of your anxious heart; lock & key I converse in ghost electromagnetically charging the table with the living battery of your pulsing fingers & my psychographic eyes, spilling salt. O you'll feel my presence spirit trumpet your knuckles. YES I got your drunken text: **EFFECT THE CHANGING LIGHT ON SAND WHAT PATIENCE WORTH.** A monkey could make more money selling macaroni art. All this fretting over the happy or unhappiness of the dead. Of *does he doesn't she do they*. Their business is their own damn zillion pored manifestation. YES you could say that *the 'spirit' is actually a representation of the collective we* but you gotta know *who*—or *what*—you're dealing with. My name means good luck & who doesn't want to trust what comes from fortune beyond? A monkey's paw. And gripped within it a brush tipped in kolinsky sable dipping in liquid gold. I can reveal your magic numbers but not their when or why. I've my own gatekeepers & though I don't always say the word you want to hear I utter no untruth. When I waffle, when I'm late to answer? Perhaps I was bored to dearth into **GOODBYE**

Horseshoe Crab

Why say fingerprint when touch heightened might leave behind dactylogram? I'm thinking of that critique with a fellow, who, late for our meeting, hungover, likened his early work to mine & *that was [my] problem. [I] need[ed] to write like this* & he thrust his new book in my grandiose & archaic hands. As if I wrote how I wrote for—or in spite of—him & not for some living fossil like myself. Ginkgo biloba. Or trapdoor spider. No; let the horseshoe crab unapologetically be my beloved saprostomous ancestor whom I mouthpiece. Trail evidence long thought coast comber whom I'd right those overcast mornings, sword sailing scorpion discs shipwrecked upon the shore in mating season who'd etch impermanent map-makings in the shifting sleech. There is no creature dearer. But also because that ancient saucepan's twinned to the memory of my father. I heeded his advice— that acclaimed poet. After all there's only so much *Limulus Amebocyte Lysate* one can drain, only so much blood harvest before the strapped carapace mulch fields or are fed to the hogs. Then I relapsed into the moon-spewed cosmopoietic. I know I'm scraping diction. I know I'm estranging. But even at the bottom of the sea there's some company, some symbiosis. Life's short: a million years—who'll remember? The sand receives then replaces granularly the wake in which I create dawdling along dragging like a tail between my legs this walking stick

Tardigrade

You're near indestructible while I'm holding on hammer & tong. Entangled on a superconducting qubit in your tun state (which is a lateness, a hibernation of immortal sugar) you withstand quantumness, transparency between storms, mud volcanoes, deep space's depression. When asked where I'd like to visit most I've answered the Brinks & meant it. The humming aloneness. Water into honey. Virgin birth. There's speculation, you know, if we're to live there in the redness after utterly devastating this dirt & Adam's ale world, we'll need splicing of your magic gen(i)es. You, a squinting vacuum-faced octoped of a crumbled paper bag seem jovial floating about, more carnival prize than moss piglet, more hot air balloon nightmare than water bear. Which isn't meant to be harsh, it isn't an insult. I've gone days donning the same outfit. You see the flowering plants, the grains of sand, the nooks of the moon in black & white; I dream in imbroglio. You're a real biological weirdo, an unsung hero; I sit in a room noodling words my cuticles peeling. But we're not completely antithetical, you & I, we're not each other's extremes—I too've a resilient streak; even when just struggling's a struggle instead of going full dormant I await revival tentative, one slow step at a time I throttle

Bigfoot

You can green a thumb. At least I'm trying pushing pennies into the dirt. Last warm season yielded basil in spades a basket of cucumbers even one baby-head of *Citrullus vulgaris*. This year a bed of stalks, leaves ravished, the cilantro a lost cause, the summer squash yellow blooms that nevertheless floundered. Here things—shadows mostly—flicker the peripheral. When in the bayou-flooded backyard I spied the mound I first thought it stranded turtle. It wasn't until it lowered resurfaced glided then breached water that I recognized the alligator as the apex predator it was. That one afternoon after the hurricane knocked the power out & I was in a sports bra & shorts my hands gloved & dirty from weeding, hair sweat-matted & two men entered the property? Perhaps it was the gravel crunching underfoot that made my skin prickle. No. I hadn't yet heard the boots casually advancing. They claimed they knew me. Truck broke down. I'd just moved in days earlier. I'd not lay eyes on them before. The etymological tendril of Sasquatch? Salish for *wild men*

Wolf

pack wending rivers. It's like that movie—a broken soul finds himself on a bridge staring into the floe cursing the day he was born but it turns out the role he plays in the plot of things extends beyond his cells & is therefore returned. Or greeting someone who remembers you but who's a ghostspot in your memory: reintroduction. Howl stirred,/ the ice-age-carved tributaries recalibrated their paths/ banks stabilized/ pools formed/ channels narrowed/ fox mice hare multiplied/ coyotes dwindled/ regrowth scarred-over splitting bark/ those crown sharpeners the elk & red deer forsook valleys & gorges receding into hills' thin/ aspen elongated skyward/ cottonwood spurted green fingerlings/ songbirds & hawk eagle raven those birds of prey rematerialized/ bears like moving caves of obsidian gorged until dreamdrunk on bushes that berried/ the fraught with chaos began to obey/ threat anew proved integral as a drop of rain to the mountains solid in their heaving/ foliage, cones, rush of prints, nuzzle, throats belling moon/ Montana's unbanning of neck snares, baiting, spotlight night-hunting, lengthening of trapping season/ bloodshed spilling/ the wolves are bending rivers

Bloodhound

Broom eared drippy jowled droopy lidded high octane nose with a mutt attached crooner canoodling *roo* & *bay* on the only planet not named for a god—theirs is the only animal evidence admissible in court. Disregarded is the blinking goldfish bubbling *mer-der-rer*. Out the window goes the parrot's Sherlock Holmesing *Rwah the butler did it!* Unrelenting when it comes to following a prickly scent over the river & through the woods since the Middle Ages trailing rabbit boar deer then in Whitechapel tracking O Jack the Knife Mack the Ripper. No doubt Barnaby & Burgho would've tailed the on-the-lam slasher had those bumbling constables on patrol left the crime scenes unmolested. Would've fleeced out that possible barber red-handed, their Hades-echoing howl scattering lambs silently ambling. The way Remi helped recover those in the wandering stage of dementia with a piece of gauze &or how Fred located missing 6-year-old Kinzleigh & her kidnapper father in a barricaded outbuilding in Tennessee &or how in his skull & crossbones collar nostrils quivering *decomposition dog* Radar identified the concealed decaying bouquet of human remains in a car trunk. It's taken decades but they've finally named (though I won't) Nancy Noga's killer

Rabbit

Vertebrae of light, belly to plaster, spine to threshold. I wasn't planned I was mistake. An accident my mother corrected. Once thought I was knocked-up though I was still a virgin. Once confused pro-choice & -life thinking the *life* meant was not of the seed but of the woman. What it is to be exploited, splayed. To say your name twice first thing first day of the month's to invoke a string of luck. Fuck-zealous forebringer of spring & renewal, surveying 360° everything—but taking for granted what's at the tip of your nose. Time my father cupped you in his hat, saved from the blades of the mower? I didn't know your other meaning that day I told my mother I found you—pet some lover'd gifted me—limp in your cage. She thought I was speaking in tongue. *Dead* as metaphor, as secret code. S.C.O.T.U.S overturned Roe V Wade June 24, 2022, skinning women of bodily autonomy. Lunar & underworld augury, demiurge lascivious & fecund. Renaissance emblem of purity & faith unquestioning. Resurrection. Constant state of alert. Low humming while circling. Crowing barking or howling midnight. Warren is a sign. Trancing's traumatic. Pounding. Heart. Is a sign. Digging's innate. But paw stomping. Thumping. Tapping. Is. Warning. *Something* drove Mary to that origin story. I watershed that summer the usual blood rope of thorns I ravished the garden

6EQUJ5

As if centuries they've been in this frosted lavender pasture, malachite grass rustling their ankles, masticating fat nostrils dripping emitting leviathan moos waiting to materialize—the bovines twist their necks to gaze abyssally back at you. Quasiqueasy you ingurgitate cream slush from a carafe, cool air tentacling out of the icebox' ajar door—your thoughts like the outrageous halogen language of flowers. Just another day in the life of a primrose eater strolling along a lotus path, the ruins in ruins. Is it because *a particle's defined by its particular vibrational pattern & that pattern's defined by the shape of the space in which it vibrates* that you mistake nightingale for the chariot of Apollo? Cloud roar, then a helix of light wowing the horizon. This is how rapture should feel. A being devoured by echo feeling. A bubbling behind the eyes, then bumbling along the ceiling, the roof peeling away, a parade of disentangling objects, the miscellanea of your life you've become the grand hoopla of, bobbing towards Pluto. If it's not calcium- but salt-crystals which make anyone's bones breakable, what makes your skeleton feel like a cage of glass? It's too late steering through the outermost pickles of space when it occurs to you—*funny, there're no farms around here for days—so why these levitating cow pies, why these burning eyes drowning me in a milky way?*

Velvet

Because I've doused my wrists in *Exit the King* & bring them supplication-wise to my face loopingly as if I could *closer*. Because sheepsy wolvesy Beethoven's playing on Pandora. Because I'm performing an exorcism on the closet & what was within lays bare over bed stitched with dog hair. Coleworts twice sodden. Cockleshells all in a row. *Art is very instinctive* declares Rosten-Edwards. In the '90s I wore you feline suited. Neon-wigged & *in velveto*, didn't I think myself queenly pussyfooting into those guillotine nights? Inspiration drawn from Peg Bundy & Hades. It's not just the dust bunnies among the skeletons I'm after. Damnit I cried last night watching *Queer Eye*. Because *Stocking Lady* & damnit *wacky fashion sense* & damnit *overdressed & underclothed*. Because in a fantasy I'm as reflective as an idea eeling behind the eyes especially crushed & Zirconian as March rain. Navigating dusk I turn on the mid-lights, those soft get-you-bys. I was intent you'd be skirt split to saddlebag, tube-top over-floweth. A text or two later—your Shane's second piss catheter. Him constipated from Chemo meds. You can't go back & it's a blessing as much as a curse. Scarf cloaking shoulder, I am adorned—I wear you; but you—you wear me out

Diamondback

What's absent in the time-elapse video of your kind minding your own low business slithering in & zipping out & noodling around your forest floor den scavenging for something to swallow is the trickling water dry leaves scuttling cement reverberation of your rattles. Ultrasonic noise that before it's heard raises nape hairs. Even recorded in song & not consciously alluded to that buzz'll strike the limbic system between the shoulder blades with vinyl ether. It's why you're equated with the symbol of transformation: to the power that rises from the base of the spine, bodily place where I've a trampstamp of dripping barbed wire. And if you believe the myth one body coiled another at the sloughing of precious fruitlight until it wasn't only mouth of the ox that was bitter-sweetly thrice bitten. Meaning innocence wasn't the first mislaid thing back in that parapsychological garden. Here song the bells. When I go to hell it'll be a returning though I'll not say what I have or have yet slickening—*colubrem in sinu fovere*—shed

Parroting

All I did was write down the world.

A poem mustn't ever be frivolous. A poem is about a thing the way a cat is about a horse. The poem must not apologize for itself. It begins in obsession. We're all repressing something. Silence is a complete thought. There is no such thing as an afterlife. The mind makes associations. Where is my reader now? Who do you think you are now based on who you were? Life isn't lived in theory. Past agitates present. There'll never be another Dickinson. What's left is lumber. Delicate equilibrium. You can't have a breakthrough without something getting broken. Poetry happens in an in-between space: a light that draws you into the swamp where you die. Change the polarity of the shadow. What might we do when we don't quite understand. Every poem is subject to interpretation. All speech is context. All writing is propaganda. Why do I feel like I failed? Why didn't you call?

Incubus

Gaping frozen in the bed I watched myself through the wall of the monastery-cum-artist-retreat walk down the hall, twin head turning to glance back at itself. My voice strangled so that I screamed a scream mouthless & unheard as the room transformed into something out of a King movie or a Keatsian poem, time unmoored I could hear vines curl like cellophane, crackling indigo it was as if a hoof were pressing me into the mattress the bed became a slab of marble as of a tomb I could not move except to close my eyes but that didn't erase the scene. Hours those moments lasting. When I came to light & birdsong seeped in through the window. I blushed when Tracey said *sleep paralysis* slipping me something to blunt the shapeshifting. Synesthesia & night hag. Hypnopompic hallucination as explanation. But she wasn't there days later, when, still unable to eat, I out-of-bodied & rose to the ceiling feeling what the spirit must approximate. My material-self bed-bound beside my wife, my wife dreaming unawares—so slowly I lifted closer to the roof of that shelter, I'd to crane toward daybreak lest my nose brush eggshell. Lest I kiss the moon of that plafond. Lest I ghost into ghost

Gumby

True, stretched by your heartstrings you never know what you might morph in or out of. *Massaging of the eye cells*. What how you move is called. *Titular green clay humanoid character*. Your gender plastic. Which's got me thinking about my baby shower. Not weather phenomena raining newborns but a churchy basement luncheon where my mumzee-to-be sat in a chair opening lavender & yellow presents. Not a sniff the diaper party where you pin a happy face on a paper vagina but an afternoon of punch bowls & homemade macaroni salad. Setting woods on fire, crashing planes, petting alligators—these modern reveals reinforcing *Guns or Glitter, Ties or Tutus, Rifles or Ruffles, 'Staches or Lashes* are—I'll say it—fucking tacky. Too much presupposition. Green: chosen because it was seen as both a symbol of life & radically neutral. I wouldn't want to know, I'd relish in the mystery if ever I were to be expecting. My legs in stirrups, my new gynecologist asks what I'm using for *control*. Embarrassed—but not for why you think—I answer *Sex with my wife*

Coat of Arms

Movement from birth place to potential breeding location; echoes of displacement; shiftings glimpsed in windows: in the photo footage the arctic fox, fitted with satellite transmitter, looked pyrrhic, maverick, climacteric mid-pant, one paw raised, tongue & teeth like flashing having navigated thousands of iced miles Spitsbergen to Ellesmere in 76 days, a record. Visiting The Emerald Isle at an immigration museum I thought not of the great plumed helm & open book but of the Cheshire of a moon above the prancing hart's antlers; at Libertas' green feet I too thought not of three shells for three goats, coxcomb, a lion of fire— but rather priestly griffins. Not *Keepers of the Hound* whose motto's *History cannot be destroyed* but servant in a household of the holy. Survival of the misfittest, the reasons selfish why I left that little forsaken shithole of a town *South Annoy* for a dot of paradise at the end of the Sunshine State's archipelago. Doesn't mean I can't still miss it. Train station. Twice as many dive bars as churches. Holied plot where we interred the cremated bones of my father

Armadillo

Sympathy for you, nude minotaur of frozen ant dreams, turtledog of noon lava hungers, whom my father once chased despite chance of leprosy in the alone star state. Because you'd been glimpsed excavating graveyards believing you burrowed through casket & devoured cadaver, Tod Browning insisted you be Transylvanian pitting you with opossum & Jerusalem cricket. Consider—this was back when Edison submitted his last patent application, Nevada legalized gambling & widespread was the Great Depression. Also: although the background was not real the coach travelling the road was; *Overture to Die Meistersinger* was the opening opera; & the count's castle?—painted glass poised in front of a camera. Waiting to be abducted impaled or brow tucked to tail snowball into hell & live blissfully pifflely thereafter. Or suicidal as ever crossing asphalt just to jut your tongue into a blackhole & dine on spider. The doctors never differentiated if after his heart stopped my father was comatose braindead or vegetative—the hospital bed in the living room like a living coffin. *Nothing dies here that needs burying* screaks the desert gothic but that mirage of a man begs to differ

Platypus

Into the blender's tossed hagfish, hadrosaurid, beaver & otter. Out comes phosphorous fur, ten chromosomes instead of two, a face with a real honker. Receptors sensitive to electrical signals—so, also dash of bat? And inkling of snake?—being venomous-spurred. Sure knuckle-waddling toward stream away from some human you'll emit a low growl slinking back into the murky but otherwise you're mostly mum. And baffle still. Metronome of a heart, egg-dropping, with a bill-full of gravel you crush worms into mush. I've an extra wisdom tooth. As if you weren't Frankenstein enough you used to be giant. Puberty startled me—the hairs the odors the bubbling below the surface; eventually assumed I was bi– but've learned I'm undeniably pan–. [In my mind uttering the *–sexual* implies sticky bodies fixed in contactual engagement & what radiates out of me does so first from the chest then the third eye then that hot center of (ecstatic) creation (my platy–) so I prefer it fragmented.] The day Po called to say she was in a relationship with a woman I think my father thought I'd be (at least) shocked. But heart mirror heart I recognized the familiar. Unshaved legs, slight upper lip shadow, eyes of mischievous twinkle, Nick (born Sherry) never said *trans* so we didn't either, said *Twisted Sister; Wet Vagina* instead of *West Virginia*; proved rose by any other butch is as water off a butch back does—that we're all vaster than the sum of our pieces

Turtle

I've a dove trove of reasons not to leave the house. Devils. Pollen. Ghosts pouring tea. A microcosmic orchard slimes my Sudoku back. The sound inside my own thinking like a pencil sharpening. Sometimes a window's confused with a landscape & vice-versa so that you're never really sure if you're gazing into or (with)in a frame. Think fly on a mirror. Or an underwater orchestra's drapey-form bent over violin, the violin acquiesing but yeilding more of a moan a hard kiss muffles—than music. This world like a disco ball in outerspace. Not because it glitters or reflects but because it dangles & smacks of immortaily unattainable. Which shouldn't sadden you. It's a blessing really, that nothing lasts forever. Just think how tired your bones get waiting for the bus. No better the party end, the headlights bending into the hedges leaving you to play that record one last time as you load the sink with smudged glasses, forks & saucers. I win the race inch by inch. I blink intentional like an ancient wizard. In place of pig skin—I'm a tossed skull. You may think I'm ET's sheltered second cousin but I'm jewelry box, shuffling sleeper coffin, I'm my own luggage. When you're gone what'll become of your *horror vacui*, who'll claim the stamp collection, who'll be tasked with emptying the skeletons in your closet?

Quakers/Quackers

Not to be confused with the *Religious Society of Friends* nor the unexplained sounds detected by submarines but monikers I christened the Pekin my father brought home, jesting was that night's BBQ dinner. *The duck test is a form of abductive reasoning.* In nature/nurture experiments not-yet-imprinted ducklings will follow a loudspeaker's rhythmic *Come Come* around in a pen adopting (or adapting?) blackbox as mother. Acoustic riddle why ducks don't echo. That's not true. That's urban legend. While drakes mostly whistle, growl, croak, purr, squeak, hoot or are quiet, Daisy in the dell's quack did indeed boomerang back. *A mechanical duck is still not a living duck* as proved by Vaucanson's grain snacking automaton excreting droppings. Watching TV, petting the snoring widgeon still as a decoy in my lap, I learned the sudden warmth wasn't snuggle as much as it was squirt of fresh shit. When Quakers/Quackers would flap onto the roof, I'd beg my father fetch the ladder; saddling peak inch by inch queasy with height cussing & cursing he'd hobble closer only for the avifauna to waddle just past his calloused grasp & swandive back into my arms (this, years before dreaming the dream he couldn't awake from, one eye open, the other fixed on some unihemispheric motion, incubating in the egg of his coma). Eventually we surrendered the bird to Cheesequake Park. We'd go visit but how to distinguish in the sudden swarming one beak from another pecking from our palms offering of popcorn & crushed crackers?

Confession(al)

Dee called this morning—I answered—said she didn't know who else to call we're sisters as far as we're concerned I was putting on my gloves to (continue) building a fence her voice broke & I thought of my mother having another stroke I thought about the house my father died in that she—Dee—now owned I thought the sun already was itch blazing the back of my neck thought of my mother alone. Sometimes love fails. Not just fails but is the quicksand the cartoons led us to believe was literal when all along was emotional, metaphoric, inevitable in being underfoot eventually. (Do I name him? I name him.) *Stosh* she tells me *was passed out on the couch, his phone & hair tie on the floor*—she paused—no this isn't how she told it—she said first how she found the syringe on the floor by his phone & hair tie, how she woke him in a fury & he lied. Lied. Said it was the first time since . . . & she—Dee—told him—after grabbing, insisting on seeing his arm—there was a blooded spot dear reader—she told him to *Get Out Now. Get Out.* Sometimes love struggles. Sometimes, struggles. *My daughter*—I caught—the phone breaking in & out—*I can't*—then another muted moment—me on the other end almost begging—*I'm here can you hear me I lost you*—her side static as if an avalanche of fine sand burying our words. Sometimes there is all along. Sometimes sooner is better than later & sometimes latent is better than never & sometimes someone sends you a clip of *Cry Little Sister* & you remember wanting to be alive

Walrus

I know you are but what am I?

A walrus decked in gold is better than an over-laden horse. A walrus is a walrus even if he is finely saddled. A walrus is rarely known by his ears alone. A walrus that happens to rest on a book pile is not necessarily learned. A wet walrus is nothing to be ashamed of. All is not blubber that comes from the walrus. Comfortable is he who doesn't have a walrus to groom. Don't harness the walrus & the seal together. Don't set out on a journey using someone else's walrus. Don't stop a walrus that isn't yours. Don't try to drive a walrus with a stick. Greatness alone is not all it takes to make a walrus. He who took the walrus up to the roof should bring it down. I am a prince & you are a prince; who will lead the walruses? If a walrus kicks you & you want to kick back, think twice. It is not true that many conformists today welcome the wet walrus in the house as a pet or mopper. Things have not taken such an ugly turn yet. It is unwise to seek wool from a walrus. Little does the walrus know about the song of a nightingale. Never stand in front of a judge or right behind a walrus. Reading scripture in front of a walrus is not safe. Shallow waters surrounding the North Pole are all right to a walrus, but not to someone who is dressed up for a party in Italy. The account of the walrus is different from that of the walrus-hunter. The walrus' best ornament lies in his nakedness. Understanding of a walrus is had by mind, eyes, bristles & so on. Walruses might fly unless the age of miracles is past. We let him in; but then he brought his walrus along, too. When a walrus climbs a ladder, he is up to something unlikely. Whoever plows with a team of walruses must have patience. You ask the walrus when it is Wednesday? You don't ride the walrus—the walrus rides you

Lazarus Taxa

What's the millionth digit of pi? Are you shy of dying? Who are the keepers of time? What are you daily afraid of? Afraid for? What's love? What makes you uncomfortable? What is intimacy? You believe in kismet? What sign are you, under whose constellation were you born? What's real? Did you know Lopadotemachoselachogaleokranioleipsanodrim-hypotrimatosilphiokarabomelitokatakechymenokichlepiko-ssyphophattoperisteralektryonoptekephalliokigklopeleiolag-oiosiraiobahetraganopterygon is a fictional fish dish containing (but not limited to) honey, thrush, boiled-down wine, shark head & sea hare pounded together, topped with blackbird & seasoned with giant fennel now extinct? What's your kink? What do you smell like? How many languages do you speak? I mean will your tongue get you killed? Has a wall ever not been political? Have I struck a nerve yet? Is this a poem? Is this? Can you read my limbic system? Is it warm in here? I mean does this echo? Has anyone ever told you you remind them of someone else? What's that in the corner? Did you know solitude contains mostly vibrational water? Have you ever dreamt you ate a giant marshmallow & awoke still in your grave-cloths only to find the stone door opened & your pillow missing? Whose backwards dog is this, whose retrograde god? Who said, *I hate questions; tell me what you know?* Do you believe in reincarnation? The soul immortal? What makes you—what? Oh; the first question? Yes, I'll repeat it: *what is the millionth digit of pi?* Why; yes; that's correct how'd you know: the number most alone

Yak

Kayak-awkward obligatory end of the fauna alphabet juggernaut, you make me want to be cleverer. But it's not enough to jabberwocky language is it it's never enough to be flyback on grape sugar. Frankly you're strawback-breakingly beautiful the way cows are when they're jaywalking in misty thistle. Your skyjack sternum. Your johnnycake eyes. Actually you seem the embodiment of refined melancholy—not a killjoy but the way a squeaky balloon is after desire, like milk before it sours. You sir or madam are the type of baggywrinkle creature a chimneystack would hire as a garden hermit. It's a real job you know, strolling among yellowjackets, stickybeaking into the affairs of others, offering cockneyfying counsel to the monkeyflowers. If you don't knowledgeably know the answer just backtalk shit up: *Sunset licketysplits through the eye of need lackadaisically on daisy dazed days like these; The peachest hour for blackberrying is between Twinkies & Borsht; & Yes that I'm a prehistoric cabbage you may be unshakably sure.* I mean if you could talkity-talk backity-back. If you could talkity-talk backity-back, we could picnic backkicking coke-a-colas, me chewing the hay chatterboxing jabbering popinjaying windjammering palavering blatherskiting about that time I almost Baker Acted myself while you buckayro in your hairshirt tongue-clicked nada about it. When I said *I didn't not get nothing* I meant I got something

Phoenix

Tricky this soft sleeve business, stealing from anteroom to anteroom to final bow. My doppelgänger pyromancer in the corner holding one struck match, lit to unlit. It's like they say—where there's smoke there's bound to be illusion engulfing the memory of two feather-roses sudden & crying out. Where there's sarcophagus: voice fire. I listen for what blooms in the outer field. Underside bruise in color. Hot streak, shudder then glimpsing the invisible. In the Bethany story the self-proclaimed savior waits before visiting during sickness to perform his covariance publicity stunt so the man named *God has Helped* purposefully dies. What of that wax-winged boy falling antisunward? As if faking *Lazarus taxon* sometimes after absence a glitch in the fossil record. Of a flame gutter means to spit; to sputter. Must a change in one be associated with a change in the other?

Quagga

Quagga logic: *The Quagga is a Quagga because of the way it looked, & if you produce animals that look that way, then they are Quaggas.* What of what was here—how reconcile the mind of the lost, the gone's hungers? How can the resurrected be what it was before it wasn't, how to return from the dead unchanged? For surely something is exchanged between dimensions, between blades of sward? Deprived of tender harem. Of another grooming her. The only living one photographed—captive in a zoo. Here she comes into startling stereoscopic focus out of cobweb. Wild grass eater, phenotype, vanished plains zebra, here she haunts magic lantern & veld. To step in or out of the picture—couldn't I imagine bristle of field against my pushing palms, or eavesdropping on moldering fruit in conversation with plattered bones? Jurassic moths glitched like telegrams from extinction, supposedly. Who's to say energy can't portal time & manifest distinguished like coal that is coal & simultaneously tooth of diamond? Quagga ultralogic: *I am returned from air like memory from a tomb, I stink of the musk of the afterlife, in the softrain my hooves pound the ground leaving imprints of my crossing*

Venus (Infers)

> *A gay couple & a lesbian couple are going on vacation—*
> *who gets there first? The lesbians because*
> *they do 69 the whole way while the gays*
> *are still home packing their sh*t.*

My cradle-snatcher wife & I decide (again) not to know each other in public on our next milk of the birds trip. I predict we'll be terrible at it we'll be so gappy (gay happy) getting away she won't even be able to keep a chapsticked straight face (*nuk-nuk*) sidling up to where I've already sauntered red mouthed wearing something ridiculous & drapey, musked in flora carnal, earrings dangling almost scything collarbone her donning white shirt untucked in jeans those high heel sneakers. Maybe atop her new crop a hat—the dust knocked off, rim bent Daddyish. Our May-December blushes usurping, new wrinkles upholding. A Beyoncé Norah Jones Nancy Sinatra kinda weekend. Olives might be involved. And rendezvous of bubbles. Pajama party sans jammies à la afternoon delight, a little slap & tickle. Glazed-over after, gazing ceiling's wicked zodiac, that delicious haunting silence subsiding. Redress. Elevator downstairs. Early dinner. Where disheveled we'll disappear in plain view reborn as Mrs. & Mrs. Who & Whomever & no one will dare fucking mistake her for my mother

Elephant

Dali's stork-legged desire, beast temporal, sugar apple: yours is a ruminating mind, certain moths sip from the pools of your sad yes eyes, you crush the couch when you sit on it. It may be your ears' silhouettes which differentiate Savanna from Forest but it is your banloca—Old English for mineralized tissue—which hears. You've humming vigils & mourning rituals, you'll zigzag shrub to bush to conceal your tusks from poachers, in caves the discovery of your giant skulls gave rise to the myths of cyclopes & ogres. What'd I know of you singular in your epiphany white hillish, cartoonlike talking *Batyr/ good/ fool/ bad/ give/ water/ yes*. That so inclined you might wave a flag, pick-pocket, paint, drum, or fire a gun. That once you stalked ancient battlefields as living tanks. Once you were served sliced as dinner in Paris. And once twice-hung from a crane. Your once fur-coated flank not the powdered leather I'd imagined but bristled. Not cotton candied but still a sweetness like hopsbreath to your rank. At that small town carnival I rode you while you, chained at your ankle, paced crop circles in the dirt. If you weren't incarnation. If you couldn't fly. If you were Lethe & not some lake of remembrance I'd drown my sorrows in the murk of you

Nudibranchs

Mostly harmless mermaid ghost. I fragment at your clown marigold dancer sea rabbit florescence, flounder at your dragon. Digit-backed jentacular carnival sushi swimming through abstraction. As if the microscopic world were magnified & drowned such, & therefore what movement into intimacy. My wife & I are going to the sea. I'm sizzling for Eden of pineapple rings, bedroom shipwreck, footprints in space—so I'm packing books & bathing suits, capes & toys, spiked slippers & a bit of the unknown. Fingertips of mathematics paralleling along a cenotes' mouthroof. I want her to spread me marmalade then toast me. Exhausted beyond crawl, the brain lubricant, firecrackered in dopamine, oxytocin, I want me tongue-tied. Museum doors soon closing away the naked gill marbles. Leaf sheep Bubble snail Feathered anus. Emptied shell. Lost in the depths I want to confuse body of water with body of water. Unaccustomed as they'll've become to solid ground my knees might sinkhole under the water column of the showerhead. Internal rocking tethering me. Substrate of floating feeling. Déjà vu a hair before the recognition. That I may return sunburned tailbone. That I might come back electric eel

Gräfenberg Spot

Almost every woman I have ever met has a secret belief that she is just on the edge of madness, that there is some deep, crazy part within her, that she must be on guard constantly against 'losing control'—of her temper, of her appetite, of her sexuality, of her feelings, of her ambition, of her secret fantasies, of her mind.

Locker room eavesdrop: *What do you call the useless flesh that surrounds a vagina? The woman!* No purpose save pleasure. *How's a vagina like a shark? One's a fishy mankiller the other lives in the sea!* Actually . . . a woman's natural lubricant shares the organic compound squalene found in the apex predator's liver. Little man(!?) in a canoe, pudendum pendulum, purple bean. If you drag a shark backwards by its tail you will kill it, flooding its gills. Sword sheath key latch touch or tickle. Ovary the size of an almond. Wishbone & Jaws-brain-shaped, uterus the size of a pear. But iceberg-like the clit may be vaster than imagined: pea or gherkin pickle. Devil's teat for soul-sucking. Divining tool for IDing witches. Despite red drops in the ocean there's no evidence linking menstruation & Megalodon attacks. *Never do anything to a clitoris—with your teeth—that you wouldn't do to an expensive waterproof wristwatch.* Lotto grotto of 8,000 nerve endings on the interior roof at 12 o'clock. Ageless boneless open-eyed sleeper. Tonic immobility. *What's the difference between a clitoris & a bar? Most men have no trouble finding the bar. What's pink & slippery? Pink slippers.* Panties in the window insisting *It's Not Going to Lick Itself.* Rosebud. Tootsie Pop. Briny brainnut. My sweetly bitter cherry pit

Yet(i)

Dark matter explosion. Shockwave of magnetic field. Submarines prowling oceans. I think of the screen's imbroglio just past acquiesce into hesitance. The sculpture *lo Sono* which only exists *in the mind of its creator* sold for 15,000 euros. This isn't the first time someone's paid for something which cannot be beheld. *Dog-skin of Hades*, Emperor's new robes. Not unlike snowflakes gleaned under a microscope tears have their own vibrational pattern idiosyncratic to the emotion from which they've sprung: overwhelmed does not look like happiness does not look like sadness does not look like love or mourning. X tells me her niece is back in the hospital after her body began responding to a phantom brain tumor. To be undone. That a woman be ground to salt for glancing back—. The mass in my breast obscure as blips. Also once withheld from human ocular comprehension: Andromeda's Halo, flowers' aureoles, bird tracks traced midflight. Doesn't it suggest dissolution, melting, disappearance, those suspended weepings? *I Am* isn't Salvatore Garau's first artwork activated between synapses; see also *Buddha in contemplation*. A thing seemed isn't always. One cannot scream underwater. Love or mourning echoing Aubade. Of its immateriality the artist noted: *After all, don't we give shape to a God we have never seen?* You think we'll be a question of sustaining when more often than not we're a stash of letters to the dead

Ichthyosaurus

One has to be careful how one goes about, reading rocks.

As a baby a black cloud hung above Mary Anning. Was even lightning struck & spared though she was sickly. A Georgian girl during war curious sensible Mary Anning could read. Was autodidactic in anatomy & geology, hers a constellation of firsts—tracing pterodactyl wing to tail, unearthing the first plesiosaur fossil album leaf upon a petrified ditty, finding in belemnite those dried ink chambers—still she had trouble making ends meet. The Men scientists those authoritatives refused to admit her. Not into their Geological Society nor to her sensitive-eyed genius. They whom procured her uncovered, cleaned, prepared, & identified specimens gave her nil credit in their prestigious scientific papers. They whom made things as they imagined them & not as they found them, touting her Ichthysuarus was crocodile roaring about on a spree far from where it should geographically be. Mary disagreed. Fully articulated the rushes are strangely, devil's fingers, snakestones, verteberries gleaned uncannily. Even when Cuvier announced his mistake of claiming her find a fake they disinclined to invite her, prattling amongst themselves patting each other's back. They whom continued sucking her brains. Then upon her death as if merhorses hoisting clam shell Venus ossified her *usefulness* in glass. Afterthought stained portal of mercy among Holy Grail vision, the war slain, the wealthy sea merchant—pane that let light in & looked upon her grave but obdurate does not open

Lobotomy

Soda coda tart shade abandoned piano in ocean water. Not gibberish but riddle. *I'm removing the bone flap* the doctor announced flatly her gloved hands abracadabraing my skull's lock. *What word starts & ends with E but only has one letter? Or what can go down a chimney when up but not up a chimney when down? What do you put into a water barrel to make it lighter?* Trepanning's trickster squid bats & gargoyle monkeys flute the room. As if it weren't all critical lateral as if I could splice con- & divergent thoughts. *Inserting endoscope.* More culling more mining. Up & down my spine a pulley system, imago, a glass saw hawing along breath. I could no longer uncurl my tongue. Here sky metals future unnoticed. Sacrament meant scar. *This is a procedure to treat problems in the brain & surrounding structures.* Not believing in ghosts is self-denial. *Here is the tainted.* You'd think I'd be awash in tranquility not gooed in self-pity, I'd be sutures/stitches, bespoke sturgeon lurking nagging barracuda, what is smoke following beauty what is bleary love degenerate—but still my pleasure like meat hooks in Silly Putty. Then sharp crack of my sternum opened. *A letter; umbrella; a hole*: the koans' spell-breaker answers. The surgeon scalpels the clumpknot of my heart *(soda coda tart shade abandoned piano in ocean water)* plops it on a tray *(soda coda tart shade abandoned piano in ocean water)* & ushers away with it—*(soda coda tart shade)* every memory blighted with *(abandon–)* you

Fog

And here, the capital of suffrage, the carriage's mouth. Electrostatic haunts me. What began in decadence became many hairs, & many more hairs. Filament. We'll think we can compromise but there'll be no reasoning with the dead. They'll forget your name you'll forget I was even here. *Now that's the spirit*, the clouds say—but those misty-eyed Nimbus live in the limbo of their own salad days. We articulate the distance so often it becomes a prayer of sorts. Or a Shibboleth. Patience, a moth in the soup, glimpse of willow wisp. Clairvoyance of the minute persuasion. Funny how you can know a thing before you know it. Involuntary memory. Spontaneous cognition. Is the landscape its own animal? I almost hadn't noticed the rusty lock fishhooked, unlocked, on the gate. Also almost unseen: the lawn yawning into gardenia hedges; a stegosaurus of broken amber cobalt green & clear bottles embedded in the concrete; the thin chain-smoking woman pacing

Drone

The queen-of-most quantity greater than recommended is the difference between dose & over-. You've your own hive language independent of clock & spot for *something is burning*. My cousin Kat cleans a spoon with candle flame. It was not mistakes you enunciated but rather mist aches, stumbling back toward your golden cauldron. Violins for wings. Molasses-like bubbling in a cusp. Some moments are razor in the apple shard of amber in the stew. They can slay you. This was no longer one of them—you could call it reprieve, Narcan, an anti-buzz. Alternative apitherapy method: your acupuncture shortens withdrawal. Dilutes the desire for having wings—slang for shooting up. Thus your bittersweet nightshade touch. Because sun raw nerved the bracelet rainbow flecks splayed across surface; the result was her wrist turning over & over midair the syringe looking soft-looking

Jackal

Every day was the same: something to eat; don't get killed; try to outsmart the poison. Exiting blackthorn & slipping into the moon of a mirror like a kite. Now sun like afterlife & horseflies on his back. World before & beyond his snout of a face: desert or dumpster. Now a celebrity at this roadside zoo. They douse him with hose water. He laps from a tin bowl. Children take his picture even when he naps through teatime dreaming in wolf-pack of graveyard picnics of quince & desolation. When I fell from the roof & broke my fall with my wrist I said I broke my wrist falling. To be haunted one must only breathe

Frog

Pocket pet of witches, reincarnated child souls, most toxic augers of weather & superstitions—your midnight croaking means rain's on the way but a draught of pollywogs's a cure-all for cancer, consumption &or weakness. You taste somewhere between mermaid & chicken, you don't dole warts nor grant wishes. In the original fairy tale it's the maiden pummeling you against the wall turning you back into a prince & not her sovereign kisses. Mistake, as Homer did, Bufo for you & open the doors of astral vision. God Almighty's been sweeping you into cloud, hailing you down upon roofs & roads since Heraclides. Because yours is the first species to die out when your habitat is contaminated you are earth gauger, poison in the water's measure. How seldom nowadays a floating fleet of ships is, too few are tempests of blood, crosses, snakes & fishes; our end times reveal themselves as nuclear cataclysm, flood & drought, pandemic. Once a week you pull off your dead skin & eat it. I get it. Like some megaton explosion I too've wanted to shed self, all leg & bleating throat & reslicken primogenial. What did I know peeling you apart teasing out with scalpel your three-chambered heart but denials sweet & tribulations vile? That, & if you had wings you wouldn't bump your salientian ass every time you hopped down the street

Vulture

My s-i-l complains. Says even her shadow's ugly. That she'll never get another glass topped table. Not even a nightstand. Too much upkeep. I think the crumbs & fingerprints residual of life. Of living. But she's not interested in that. Yes I mean living. Now that her mother's passed. Her only goal to outlive the 90-year-old woman. I wouldn't say she's distraught. She doesn't say she misses her but that doesn't mean she doesn't, does it? I won't say what is & isn't because of her disease. Won't say she's suicidal. Won't say she's ungrateful. When I ask what she does all day now she says *try not to sleep*. I won't say her special talent is martyrdom & finding 10 problems for your solution. That without a liver my cousin probably won't see his next birthday. That her nephew is pissing blood because he has a tumor. Don't say you don't have the patent on cancer. I deal the cards. Raptor symbolism: death, rebirth, equalizing, perception, trust, seriousness, resourcefulness, intelligence, cleanliness &or protection. Sometimes we drink & I read her my poems but never the ones about her. When the next day she tells me she dreamt about the woman who gave birth to her but can't remember anything I can't tell her what it means

Mushroom

Why do we prize rarity & not its cousin deformity? The arbitrary unmasked is the occult science of aesthetics. I speak of the uncanny valley, wheat cake & whelk brewing between your must reeking pages—wattle. Of macro-, micro-, pelo-, teleo-, metamorphopsia & time distortion. Nature's not trying to trick you into poisoning yourself. How to cope—this daily barrenness, its glisten polish? Sometimes the only way to please a deity is disbelief. Filament to stitch the tear in heaven shut. Don't stew. Rake the leaves off the concrete sidewalk so the pathways from the saber-toothed to the throat radiate. To detect such designs, however, is not necessarily to understand them. Of being unencumbered & ushered slightly tipsy towards wreckage uncalled-for. If I bleed you gill-side on a piece of paper white spore print telltale sign you'll kill me. If unsure in foraging of the *Eat Me Drink Me*, rule out milky sap, fine hairs, spines, umbrella-shaped flowers, shiny, waxy leaves, the almond scented & taste on an empty stomach. It's ultimately best however to leave the Destroying Angel unmolested

Ibex

In one cyber world it was written: *When Thriving Ibex enters the battlefield, you get ⚡⚡ (two energy counters)* but I misread it as encounters. Historically you once numbered thousands of thousands. Now minotaur haunting figment. Springtails lived on snow fields' windblown pollen grains. The reverse rain recurving grass blades, glaze-eyed the unfurling microflowered stems. I too feel godly, I feel scientifically exact, I pull a tarot. *Each verse is an inferno. Each word is a tongue of fire. The flames of Hell burn fierce...& purify! Read on & learn the law.* Mountains transversely rigid. Classic nosed. Shadows fragmented into cloven prints in powder. *The work which a body can do in springing back after a deforming force has been removed* is one formal definition of resilience. In which silence again echoes as if a refinement of frequency distribution at the fulcrum. How becalmed you seem overlooking the pillow lavas as trophy after trophy hunter lightly touches those sweeping wild goat scimitars jutting from your poached Baphomet face

Onanism

In his rejection of ghosts St. Augustine wrote *that some visions have appeared not knowing where their bodies lay unburied.* Here gapes a wound of a self-inflected nature. Strange is nothing: nothing is strange. A gothic mirroring. This was flesh, no ghost, blood coursing veins & gripdeath. This moment not rotating exposure. Or, quasi-uncloaked & closeheld, was fringe. Let me be clear. Of thieves, the glances. I was oblivious until my mind processed the blatant. June. End of June. The air obscene. A haze. This unknown this stranger seemingly startled by his own phenomena of volume the way one might second guess oneself & double back to the door, grab the knob & attempt its swivel. Here fingerling & floral name along this gutted hollow. Waistband pulled to plinth, the patience with which he was plumbing, unrushed, dusting himself. My privacy of knowing beauty transcends its own point of reference. Shafts of sun blading sky. Dangerous, getting close

Kkaahkkaahrowch

Both the cockroach & the bird would get along very well without us,
although the cockroach would miss us most.

I misspell you to dispel you lest you illaqueate or immiserate me. I feel you. I mean your presence. I sense you lurking then you appear like a clapperklaw magician. One you might as well be a million. Like that night you infiltrated—my panik awoke the sleeping old woman, I kontemplated arson, I slept with all eyes open. And I won't name that house whose lights only illuminated your wall-krawling dominion (nor that voyeur father's even more inappropriate behaviors). I've never broken a heart without utterly shattering it. Or: after what must be akin to devastation or betrayal or plain disgust I've not mattered for so long like the dinosaurs I mightn't have ever existed. To help jilted lovers for fifteen dollars the San Antonio Zoo will name you after a former significant other & feed hissing you to bird, reptile or mammal; I can only imagine how many Kafkaesque Flowers have been devoured. Me being offered to kingfisher, leopard gecko, hedgehog. Me flailing at the hunger. Me breaking free & nevertheless living without my head. At least long enough to be nightmare fodder, find a damp korner, & spit terror. But it doesn't have to be divorce or a split-up; just like stars one can name you after a beloved. They'll even give you a certificate. Proof of devotion, of a love hard but not impossible to kill

Lobster Shack

And since I'd already had birthday champagne when Cloris Leachman implored I recite to her poems in the smoky A & B bar I star-struck made a bunch of drunk shit up about the moon yes the moon as it was out the window smearing its creamy shimmer over the water licking the yachts salty. *Another, another* she, sober, demanded but I was a sloshed swashbuckler who'd exhausted what new newnesses there might be to say about the moon spilling moon & more moon & soon we two were ships, her raising her sails EXITward & I ferrying back to my party where I was missed but only slightly. So I drifted. Found 9-year-old me following Lupi through the wet-cold walk-in cooler where crates of crustaceans awaited their plated fates. In exchange for driving to Maryland or Delaware loading a truck with the ransacked caught Roy'd offer my father a bushel of pauper's lobster—those Chesapeake blues. My parents fought but not those nights the kitchen rank with Old Bay, newspapers splayed, flies buzzing, nutcrackers cracking sooks, nutpicks digging jimmies. Opening body. Peeling the feathery cones of deadman. The ultimate prize? Finding the poor man's caviar called *coral* in certain circles: boiled orange pearls that'd mash like moist Nerds on my tongue. Didn't I fancy myself an Ariel slurping tomalley an Ursula among the sprawled shells a little scuttlebutt queen flossing my teeth with a jagged, ragged, rubied claw

Dearest

it's a waste to save the good towels. the chocolate covered cherry. who doesn't think they've time mortal aplenty? i'm saying i'm letting go by holding on i'm following my own mourning ritual of suspended state room & open burial. unlike the tissue wrapped finch something midnight scavenged i mean to keep lucy's frame—outline of vertebrae nearing surface as if a rising from within no more than a rag i cradled. people also ask *what do you mean by emptiness what does thudded mean what is a farand?* i wished she wouldn't wake. to disappear aslumber. to've portaled vouchsafe on pink clouds o'er the prism bridge into animal heaven—that'd i'd not have to make *that* decision. v mishearing *lack of* instead of *lap of love*—it was valentine's day everything twisted—& this, on the heels of another graver grief, & so in no mood i said to lexi growling showing teeth *don't make me tell the vet it's you*. days later i visited the magnolia that shaded the kennel coffer. first cut in the cooler weather & *lucilia cuprina* acrawl, sheep-strike the fallen. sky to tomb now crowned in camellias—i was awaiting piano & clover, for the socket-sunken to stir in the slightest—the way i (& dana-gaye) (& v) hallucinated beloved kiki in her casket mirage as if stillbreathing

Another Roadside Attraction

Since the dawn of horse & buggy wheels've been pancaking critters, even the phrasing *America's roads kill unknown millions of animals a year* hair-pin bends accountability from the pedal-to-the-metal-foot to asphalt's fault. *Georgia's Brunswick Stew. Kentucky's Burgoo. Jersey's Furry Frisbees.* A study found 6% of drivers *purposefully riskily* swerved on a road's shoulder to hit a fake snake tarantula or turtle. I've run into traffic arms flailing yelling *wait-wait-wait* trying to shoo a panicked stray out of the lanes only for him to dart into the parking lot & duck under a truck—its family's truck. How he got loose they'd no clue I'm not looking for a pat on the head I'm no saint. When my aunt who'd give me a Zima then tell my father I was drinking, who never paid me to babysit but swore she would, who'd let me gun the dunes & donut the sand at the empty beach barely able to reach the breaks was diagnosed with spots on her brain I said not entirely not joking *I expected they'd find her in a ditch on the side of a road*. I buckle at bridges, pump my imaginary break bracing myself telling whoever's hands are poised at 11 & 8 o'clock to *watch-watch-watch* driving the interstate. When she was released from the hospital & hoofed it to the gas station for smokes in the middle of the night & was the victim of a hit-&-run— was it clairvoyant guilt or hindsight's rearview culpability which dumbstruck me? Never mind Shane saying she may have jumped never mind I wasn't the one behind the wheel steering—I'm still reeling

Probably Bears

When you go after honey with a balloon, the great thing is not to let the bees know you're coming.

Giant dog-cat keepers of the porridge, bumbling hollowers of the honey pot, you hug like an arm wrestler. When I clicked on *What is a fun fact about bears?* one answer was: *Adult [grizzlies] can run-up to an incredible 40 mph.* If you were here I bet you'd slash that hyphen with your 2" to 4" long bear claws. Which are not the same as those buttery almond Danishes. (Yum.) Shane's one of you. Even though he doesn't have a hairy coat (*bear back* not being the same as *bareback*) & hardly sports a mustache & doesn't wear chaps (some people wear bees which can be a pun on *beware*) his chest *is* mildly tufted—this *before* disease riddled him skin & bone & bile bag. Before he spent his days hibernating with pain & meds. I understand to bear a burden upon one's shoulders because of your strength being 2.5 to 5 times stronger than a human's—but doesn't one also bear the soul in baring it? I mean, all that weight in exposure

Undertaker

Mystery, most things—sunprints of fern leaves like squid ghosts or exoskeletons retaining memory. Sea foam garlands the crypt of Delia circa 1870 & she's not alone. These buried tombstones deemed *Unclaimed Property* stave the sieving water. Of course, what is a slat of granite to the ocean but a wafer? Reduced to a sarcophagus lid this unknown *BELOVED* crumbles at the edges disappears into dark socket & here someone now fragmented as *REST I* answers to spindrift. I'd come for some peace but find myself fixating on the gulls all throat & bladed face annihilating the French fries. From here it's hard to tell the difference between the Great Highway & conversation among rock, waves rasping shore. What is revealed & when & to whom, liminal self of moorage & brine. I hadn't considered the barnacles rocket armor spreading & fusing, wreckage of moon mouths unhinging oracles in coffins but there they were filtering the RIP in tide. Isn't that what abstraction is, language intersecting dreaming? The smoke rising from a pyre's meant to symbolically hearken the soul's ascension into the ether but I'd rather you crush my bones into zirconia or let me sleep with the blobfishes

Maggot

When asked the secret of longevity centurions tend to reply "Keep breathing."

It's cheaper to use real cadavers than fashion them out of dyed noodles & rubber. A decapitated head's brain remains conscious for 20 seconds & the still warm blood cupped from the guillotine was believed a health tonic. Rigor erectus is the name of the boner gallowed men get. Migraines, the only warning sign of an aneurysm. Pistachios like linseed oil may impetuously combust. The misbelief grubs would burst out of slabs of meat left on a table? Spontaneous generation. Nightly explosions, the Teacups haunted with dust, Disney's a *Top 10* place to scatter your loved ones' ashes. Vending machines kill more people than sharks, oceans have more plastic than plankton, mosquitoes have teeth; plagues are six-feet-deep, a horse'll eat a bird, whales drown. Sound's the last sense to fade apparently. Southpaws' lives average 3 years shorter. The doctors' chicken scratch? To blame for the demise of 7,000 people annually. Worse odds with rabies. In the last moments you may experience what's known as *Ego Chill* or the *Existential Slap*. Debridement's the art of dressing an exudating wound in gown of larva—which differs from tapeworms' absorption (bovine dining on grass after the rain, eggs in the mud, shit in the water). Instar after instar, between molts, immatures writhingly occasion the death hour making for a bejeweled exquisite corpse you may mistake in the copse as sighing

Sky Whale

A helicopter troubles above pissing spray meant to kill mosquitoes. According to *The Sun* over the course of fifty days the *Blue Whale Challenge's* group administrator assigns members daily tasks ratcheting the ante. *Waking in the middle of the night. Watching a horror film. Standing on the ledge of a tower block.* Contained within the human brain's older parts a multidimensional universe similar to the animals from which we progressed. How much wants to come full circle? Ahead of the centenary a commissioned balloon—pendulous breasted creature in the form of wingless flying sculpture—to address if we evolved differently & took to atmosphere instead of sea-returning: winged; not finned. A cetacean floats across sky as if sky were ocean while a girl shows off a leviathan outline freshly razored into her forearm flipping her middle finger. The game—as its participants call it—culminates in suicide. I think of the word *ultimately*. Of a barnacle-scarred fluke's temporary fringe of brine breaching surface then disappearing steeply below waterline

| {Pill[(ow) Talk]} Bug |

I would go as far as to say that arthropods have been eating arthropods since the dawn of arthropods becoming arthropods.

Even in trilobite fossils, evidence of cannibalism. Conspecific prey, thinning over-crowding, mistaking one's own for another's egg—who's to say? In aggressive spillover hypothesis, it's *usually* the female whom cannibalizes her mate prior to during or after procreation. It's been dog eat dog in the animal kingdom since the beginning. And in Deuteronomy 28:53-57 even the daintiest will consume her afterbirth, her newborn children. *You save yourself or you remain unsaved*. Though some devouring's metaphoric. Of regrets? I've a few I've repeated & deliberately. Others—like getting into vans or drinking the nightclub Kool-Aid—*just happened*. Sometimes I say *I'm all balled up* when confused. I've been agglomerated, conglobated, in fetal position, curling into my own inhabitance only to still be on exhibition. Some mornings my tongue was fuzz & the room fuzzier. $C_{16}H_{12}FN_3O_3$: *Circles; Carpets; Mind Erasers; Kit Kat; Cat Valium; Grievous Bodily Harm; Black Holes; Gamma Ray; Bedtime Scoop; Purple; Mad Season; Trip-&-Fall; Rope; Liquid X; Cherry Meth; Salt Water; Lunch Money; Wolfies; Roach; Rib; Forget Me; Ruffles; Roofie*. A fumbling, a barrier, an obstacle to reckon with. I've got out—*by Jove or by Job?*—by the skin of—& between—my teeth. What you don't remember can't hurt you now can it

Machine Deep Learning (Cento)

There is nothing to say *in general* about the meta-theory idea; & for any given case there is too much to say. [Take] one example of the sort of wooly thinking we are up against. Seeing things in sunlight & shadows, finding a path through cluttered terrain, fitting pegs into holes. It is obvious that it is more risky to be in some states than others. Don't feel like you have to claw your way out of an endless pile of pet hair. *We looked up from our verses like blind-folded captives,/ Sent out to seek the light; but it never came.* Most people think of robots as made of metals & ceramics but it's not so much what a robot is made from but what it does. Where real creatures are concerned, of course, we have multiple interacting changes, & no explanation at our fingertips. Some philosophers say they do not know what the thesis of determinism is. It means that the person has some desire or intention, & also has the requisite belief. Qualitative betweenness falls. But, of course, the connectionist *doesn't* stop there. I am aware that in presenting the argument as I have done, neglecting the ever-interesting varieties of case, I have presented nothing more than *[sic]* a great intricacy. The phenomenon of understanding is an ongoing series of historically embedded events. [Security] forces detained Ai-Da at the boarder & wanted to remove the cameras in her eyes

Rhinoceros

We shot you Archibald, yes, with enough dope to tranquilize Donkey Kong or any sorta 4000 lb. savage beast megafauna but only *after* your second attempt trying to skedaddle, vamoose, crash out of your enclosure. Yes, this open air grotto with its concrete mud wallow's no utopian grassland where oxpeckers preen you of earwax & pluck your ticks like snatching buttons as you, heady, catch a whiff of zebra breath but you gotta admit it's still a retreat! Are you kidding me!?! No crocs lurk here—just those jellies on tourists' feet! No poachers wanting to pulverize your horn into unicorn powder here, no siree Baldie! Alas, we have no giraffes, no wooly mammoths but didn't we, sweltering hours under the Tampa sun, offer you tubs of mashed fruits & wilting butter lettuces?! Archy what was that small 14-21 oz. brain of yours thinking?!? Arch, the grass isn't greener unless it's Astroturf. This ain't no National Geographic. Given the chance they'd make a cornucopia outta your skull! They'd skin you & stitch your pelt into purse & matching raincoat! Don't believe me?! You didn't see McQueen's hoofish shagreen lobster claw python armadillo ballerina shoes in **W**!!! All I'm saying is you may be swapping one zoo for another in your search for an Eden. Out there who'll hose you down?! Who'll scratch your back with a rake & shovel your gigantic shit & call you *Baby*?

Nightmare

If you've never thought a machine heartbreaking you've probably not seen Sun Yuan & Peng Yu's *Can't Help Myself*. If you've not thought chanting skin-crawling perhaps you've not encountered Diemut Strebre's *The Prayer*. In the letter to my younger self I write what makes me most alive as if one could usher plasma back into wound. In the letter to my older self I woke to a ceiling I didn't recognize in a room I'd never slept in before. Some people prefer the company of glass & pithy fortune. Make a music ultimately of the vacuum. Not a tinkling but a clanking of diamond & choric leaves, silver chain dropping. It all comes to cosmic radiation in the language of spirituality: I take pleasure in stripping the bed but loathe fighting the pillows back into their cases: wrath of feathers. There should be a word for the place you return to—something like *lonely drinker* or *oil oozer*. There are at least as many ways to vanish as there are to suffer &or to sing. Is it ever home if you haven't bled there?

Zero

According to NASA the sun's corona appears dustier than expected but you most acidic substance are ruled by dwarf planet Pluto. Thus you're colder-hearted. Make shadowy appearances only to vanish after. Ground, goose, & ceiling you detonate, eliminate, obfuscate. Cusp of Fibonacci crescent where time crouches onto itself. Because from you the gigantic balloon that is the universe the unfathomable singularity at the core of a blackhole the counteracting gravity. You're pretty damn vast for nothing, like an Uncle No, the existential nature of missing columns. De facto not a sentence here without you which must mean you aren't only placeholder, tortoise-shell, eye fruit square root of enlightenment, wind tomb, triangular distance but also a letter. Should we be so surprised *none* is now a common reply (at least in America) to *what's your religion?*

Flea

Remember mercy not as quality but as action. Infamous Medieval mass-rat-killer, you've been vampiring since the Mesozoic Era. When my father's cousin's neighbor's dog jumped the fence & pinned me against the siding—this was years before the fumigation candle in my bedroom sputtered over & consumed the house—I remember—I've always been dumb & intuitive I remember despite the snapping teeth hot barking the spittle in my face the Cerberus paws more than twice my size steadfasting me, my hands mittened unable to push its length from me, I remember believing *you will not hurt me*. I can love to a fault like that—while yours is a true *what-you-put-in-is-what-you-get-out*: you maul on blood, digest blood then shit rehashed blood your hatched feast on. Hadn't he just stepped into the threshold in his A-shirt, barefoot, beer in hand? I won't say there was something pudding stone or honeysuckle about him. Micro-sideshow artists rattling tambourine, fiddling fiddler, strumming banjo or circus actors tightrope walking, seesawing, shooting from a cannon. No mind you might be tethered to a leash of spun gold or fixed in place with a dot of glue or not even there, a figment of magnetic suggestion. My father intervened. Anyone present would say *unprovoked*. *Target*. Me. Later running. In the. Dead-end street. Playing. I don't know. Late fall or early. Spring who recalls? Dregs of snow. Maybe. I imagined. Canine. Incisor. The animal eye flicker, familial

Axolotl

Perhaps in 1839 Johann Jakob von Tschudi meant to crown you *blunt mouth*. Neoteny regenerator. Ideal human model. *Water monster*. Of tiger. Not vampire cat or Victorian slang for prostitute—but rarest salamander with poppy seed eyes. Found only in one complex of lakes, one of which no longer exists. If noon's the vortex hour where Poseidon anagrammed into poisoned & marsupial into I am a slurp then anagram reinvented itself into a rag man. Meanwhile you just float timorous carnivorous in your bath, sorta smiling—as if you've got this primitive streak business all figured out—hypnotic buoy. You've a Sea Monkey Cum Cabbage Patch Kid verisimilitude to you that makes me think of that extraterrestrial & chimpanzee couple holding their hybrid alien-monkey (human) baby. (Where'd you think we came from?) To've syntax & imagery work in equal measures. Like the spirit of the staircase glancing over its chilled shoulder. Or the threat display of a devil's flower mantis

Fisher Cat

> *An artistic spirit such as yours naturally requires a certain amount of luxury, & why shouldn't you live in elegance, have oysters & champagne as much as you like, drape yourself in silk, velvet, & sable, & when at home, lounge in your ermine upon an ottoman?*

An awful sound, the worst sound—the red fox mistaken for your screaming. Are solitary except in breeding season. Caterwauling blacksmith pounding metal, really you're a ferocious weasel taking on porcupine & lynx. I've been told to peel my pink & let the mouser have my kisser. I've been tiaraed vulgar kitten & still strutted down an alley looking like bait by virtue of existing. Been wolf-whistled *God damn girl you are voluptuous* by a stranger twice my age my first time in the city. My freshman year a senior leered *While you're down there* as I genuflected to pick up a pencil. A male mentor admonished *Well you're not exactly demure*—he meant my profanity but his eyes watched the wind flick my vintage dress at my heart. And maybe I looked poachable that day strolling down Duval Street with my longer in the tooth—that is, cougar—wife, our hands not entwined when a pack of drunk frat boys passed & one snorted *Jesus Christ look at those ham hocks!!* I snapped like a bra strap, forwent the high road, hackles raised lips smacking yowled *Oh yeah you chauvinist pig come pet my silky pelt I fucking dare you* before Cheshiring

Centipede

A literal cold-blooded serial killer hardwired for hedonistic murderlust carnage-thirsting past satiation severing limbs & decapitating prognathic heads grislier than Vlad the Impaler. But in the devour-or-be-devoured dead of night where survival hinges on Darwinian precision the line between premeditation & psychopathic instinct's more complex than either be quickest to inject the nerve twitching juice or find oneself oozing spoils, isn't it—when also buried within that tongue-shaped segment of your midbrain's a neuron kernel containing *a form of consciousness?* That just as if threatened earwigs'll fake their death & honeybees'll buzz delightedly if given certain sugar, you've some sense of yourself in this world, of your suffering or bliss. Despite your profusion of little legs, venomous jaws & bodily segmentation I imagine you don't imagine yourself grotesque of heart, a squicky monster but rather some incarnation of destruction doling necessary chaos, an alien gladiator of evening. If I'd a transmigration of soul I'd like to think I'd be a comely widow as she looks in shadow, that cinched in my red corset I'd have the obsidian temperament of a sausage grinder xylophoning toward you. That in our *danse macabre* embrace it'd be *you* iron-maiden-cradled enduring my paralyzing siphoning kisses, I'll drag *you* higher up my ugly ganglion web, my silk binding unrushed, I take my sweet grain by grain time—darling only a widow survives a widow's bite

Zwitterion

Is choice ever not a luxury? Because she'd been used to keeping her own company my mother said motioning vaguely towards me in the hall her breathing all softened grunts & troubled huffs: *You're like a ghost crawling the walls.* Only a fool severs down trees in search of the forest. It's a mistake to believe the thicket whistling *I can't tell you how you enter me* or to inter bulbs in winter. *Is poetry anything other than craft practice & therapy? Eternity* also being a hypo-allergenic fragrance. I'm heartsick for the déjà vu of remembrance. I believe in placebos. I take chances. The way tongue revisits a tooth's empty socket I've set pocket-fires, I've flown dreaming. In the absence of an anisotropic crystal positioned in plane with an optic axis the field waxes. Strange smell suddenly emanating. Content & form—a pained negotiation. To creature structure. So much of life happens internal. Power outage. Busted pipe. Listening to the house rife with shutting down startles me worried. How among snake grass & timothy the horses manage the impossible quality of capnomancy gnawing straw. Once a fishmonger cleaved the paws off a scrawny pussycat instead of tossing some mackerel scraps. The miserly bastard. These fruitflies all puncture & rapture. All my demons unslakeable. To talk clearly here is to take sky between your teeth. You rake my subconscious raw. Of the seven devils I'm mostly Asmodeus. Of heaven's guards, I'm the one hanging in front of the 7-11, fallen. A special kind of tortured, the anguished. The laws of physics speak the binding equations. I wished like I missed—often & deeply. Yes I'm trying to get you to love the inner salt of me but only because I'm lonely in the head

Sestina

It's threading ether; one hand bound the other raveling the strappado binding; nest as expression of its builder: haystack macramé branches, papier-mâché cocoon of masticated petal, tunneled cathedral of mud & clay; all that is worshiped; lies one tells oneself effete with conviction; data rendered in blood-ringing; all heightening of existence; an invitation, a welcome to the fall; covering with leaves the pitfall to trap the panther in sepulcher with pretense; the gelding needing prodding; rosehip & bullwhip; a key you mislay; a key you mislay in snowfall; censorship of the unrequited as love cannot bother; the clothes ever in need of folding; future tense hyper-; slayed heart on display hoarding its sunfall; it's wish & wisher; rearranging the viceroyship of words into godship; that hand as it is belay that it belie that it befall notwithstanding; dumbfounding, smashing into the corner with your hip or finger with hammer; the paleorainfall returning as a wedding in Hades Queen consort of the garden, Hortense, uses to bedew the tulips among the bees' swordplay; bewitchery & bewitcher; the beginning of the ending cointense with the ending of the beginning; ship passing ship, the night ocean an ocean of virelay; it's the falling in love with her the precise moment you kill her

Zonkey

Thus we anomaly upon the coral-billed black swans as they Loch Ness across pond nipping their wavery reflections. Fate's always been pickled. Sometimes for their fickle pleasure the gods demand of us inanities—think virgin heave-hoed into the volcano's belly or tearing the baby in two. In this instance, a thread buried in a haystack of needles you must extract with your teeth because. What is the nature of a question but a questing? Zedonk aka zebrass aka zebronkey aka zebadonk aka zenkey aka deera—you are all the crapshoot chromosomal proof anyone needs of lightning striking where it's once before struck, kick quitclaim in the gut. Meanwhile high in their bed of ambrosia between orgies the deities look down the bridges of their noses through the stratosphere at our spinning marble. Imagine: the lips pierced & bleeding, the tongue a tongue of quills as at last the last splinter overthrown, the string a string enshrined in razor fishbone shatterment, a helix of red hair. Odd child fret not; we are all galactic spaghetti phenomena puppeting the particle light. If we're lucky enough to be alive aren't we lucky enough?

Notes

The word "Zoodikers" is defined in *Ware's Victorian Dictionary of Slang and Phrase* as "God's hooks—hook sometimes being hooker."

CAConrad quote from their article "On the 10th Anniversary of the Disappearance of America's Anti War Movement While the Wars Rage On," *Jewish Currents*, Feb. 7, 2020.

Carol Conroy quote from her poem "Children of Gullah," published in her book, *The Beauty Wars*.

Zymurgy
Epigraph by Marianne Moore.

Dodo
"Marie" refers to Marie Howe; quote taken out of context during a panel at The Key West Literary Seminar, 2015. "One Human Family" refers to my friend and activist JT Thompson's motto, which the City of Key West adopted as their official philosophy in 2000. "One Human Family" bumper stickers are available for free by sending a business-sized self-addressed envelope to: One Human Family, P.O. Box 972, Key West, FL 33041.

OUIJA
The pun "What Patience Worth" is also meant to invoke the poet from beyond the grave, as revealed on July 8, 1913, through medium Pearl Curran. Poem also invites the spirit of W. W. Jacob's "The Monkey's Paw" into the séance room.

Wolf
Informed by Brodie Farquhar's article "Wolf Reintroduction Changes Ecosystem in Yellowstone," from the Yellowstone National Parks Trips website, June 22, 2023.

Bloodhound
In memory of Nancy Noga.

6EQUJ5
The statement "a particle's defined by its particular vibrational pattern & that pattern's defined by the shape of the space in which it vibrates" is borrowed from string theory, exact source lost.

Velvet
"Exit the King" is the name of a scent from the fragrance house Etat Libre d'Orange. "Queer Eye" refers to the fashion-centric reality TV show originally called *Queer Eye for the Straight Guy*. "Stocking Lady" was an unflattering nickname the neighborhood kids called me behind my back freshman year.

Diamondback
Inspired by the video footage and article, "'Nightmare Material': Timelapse Shows Rattlesnakes Get Rowdy After Dark In Vermont," by Mark Price, Nov. 12, 2021. The phrase "*colubrem in sinu fovere*" is Latin for "to embrace the snake in the bosom."

Parroting
Epigraph by Jennifer Grotz, said during a poetry reading; body of poem gleaned from years of writing workshop notes.

Gumby
The phrases "massaging of the eye cells" and "titular green clay humanoid character" are from the Wikipedia entry for "Gumby."

Coat of Arms
Informed by Meilan Solly's article "A Young Arctic Fox Traveled From Norway to Canada in 76 Days," *Smithsonian Magazine*, July 3, 2019. "South Annoy" is a bastardization of the city South Amboy in central New Jersey, where I grew up.

Platypus
In loving memory of Nick Trovato.

Quakers/Quackers

"The duck test is a form of abductive reasoning" is borrowed from Wikipedia's entry "duck test" in which it is reasoned "if it looks like a duck, swims like a duck, and quacks like a duck, then it probably is a duck." The "nature / nurture experiment" refers to ethologist Konrad Lorenz's work with goslings and imprinting, Wikipedia page "Imprinting (psychology)," and information gleaned from Grzimek's *Animal Life Encyclopedia*. Exact source for the phrase "a mechanical duck is still not a living duck" is lost. The language describing the vegetative state in the poem was informed by Lidia Wasowicz's observation: "Birds often sleep with one eye open and half their brain awake. In scientific circles, this is known as unihemispheric sleep," *Central Connecticut State University*.

Walrus

Epigraph is from Paul Ruebens's character Pee-wee Herman and is punning with the Beatles's phrase "I Am the Walrus." The poem itself is a found poem from oaks.nvg.org.

Lazarus Taxa

Gleans information from Wikipedia and *National Geographic* article "Sciencespeak: Lazarus taxon" by Riley Black featured on Feb. 2, 2015.

Yak

Alludes to the John Ashbery quote, "A yak is a prehistoric cabbage: of that, at least, we may be sure."

Quagga

"The Quagga is a Quagga because of the way it looked, & if you produce animals that look that way, then they are Quaggas," alludes to a quote by Reinhold Rau referenced in his obituary in *The Telegraph* on Mar. 24, 2006.

Venus (Infers)

Epigraph is a "joke" I heard as a child well before understanding my sexuality;

title is a pun from *Venus in Furs and Selected Letters of* by on Leopold von Sacher-Masoch.

Elephant
Gleans information from Stacy Conradt's Sept. 9, 2008, *Mental Floss* article, "The Quick 10: 10 Famous Elephants."

Nudibranchs
Borrows language from Wikipedia's "Nudibranch" entry.

Gräfenberg Spot
Epigraph is from activist and author Elana Dykewomon, "Notes for a Magazine," *Sinister Wisdom: Surviving Psychiatric Assault & Creating Emotional Well-Being In Our Communities*, Issue 36, Winter 1988/89. "Never do anything to a clitoris…" is inspired by the quote, "Never do anything to your partner with your teeth that you wouldn't do to an expensive waterproof wristwatch." by P. J. O'Rourke from his book published in 1983, *Modern Manners: An Etiquette Book for Rude People*.

Yet(i)
Salvatore Garau's quote, "After all, don't we give shape to a God we have never seen?" is from Peony Hirwani's June 4, 2021 article "Italian Artist Sells 'Invisible' Sculpture For More Than £12,000" in *The Independent*.

Ichthyosaurus
Epigraph source unknown. Poem borrows language from Marie-Claire Eylott's *Natural History Museum* article, "Mary Anning: The Unsung Hero Of Fossil Discovery," as well as from Charles G. Leland's translation of Joseph Victor Scheffel's poem "The Ichthyosaurus."

Ibex
The quote "When Thriving Ibex enters the battlefield, you get ⚡⚡ (two energy counters)" is taken from Magic: The Gathering's Thriving Ibex card.

Onanism
Poem inspired by quote from St. Augustine of Hippo: "... that dead men have at times either in dreams or in some other way appeared to the living who knew not where their bodies lay unburied ..."

Kkaahkkaahrowch
Epigraph by Joseph Wood Krutch.

Dearest
The series of questions "what do you mean by emptiness what does thudded mean what is a farand?" are auto-generated.

Another Roadside Attraction
Title taken from Tom Robbins's novel.

Probably Bears
Epigraph from *Winnie the Pooh* by A. A. Milne. Poem is for Shane Mason, who, when asked his favorite animal (after cats and dogs) answered, "Probably bears."

Maggot
Some information gleaned from mondestuff.com. Epigraph paraphrased from *Restorative Health* article "Live to 100–Health Secrets of Centenarians."

Sky Whale
Poem references information about the internet phenomenon, Blue Whale Challenge, from Wikipedia and Ant Adeane's Jan. 12, 2019, article "Blue Whale: What Is The Truth Behind An Online 'Suicide Challenge'?" featured on BBC. Poem also alludes to Patricia Piccinini's hot air balloon sculpture, *The Skywhale*.

|{Pill[(ow) Talk]} Bug|
Epigraph from Live Science article "World's Oldest Known Case Of Cannibalism Revealed In Trilobite Fossils" by Cameron Duke. Quote "You save yourself or you remain unsaved" is from Alice Sebold's memoir, *Lucky*.

Machine Deep Learning (Cento)
Borrows language from *The Philosophy of Artificial Life*, *The Philosophy of Artificial Intelligence*, *Free Will*, and articles on AI by Ashley Strickland, CNN's Wonder Theory science newsletter, Nov. 27, 2021; and the article "Meet The Robot That Can Write Poetry And Create Artworks" by Hannan Ryan.

Rhinoceros
Poem inspired by Dana Treen's May 6, 2010, article "Jacksonville Zoo's Archie The Rhino Spends Morning On The Lam," *The Florida Times-Union*.

Fisher Cat
Epigraph from *Venus in Furs and Selected Letters of* by on Leopold von Sacher-Masoch.. The phrase "An awful sound, the worst sound" is taken out of context from Anna Long's YouTube video "Fisher Cat Sounds."

Centipede
References Carrie Arnold's May 5, 2022, article "The Surprisingly Sophisticated Mind of an Insect," *Noema*. The phrase "comely widow" is taken from serial killer Belle Gunness's lonely hearts ads. Some language in the poem is also indebted to Gordon Grice's *The Red Hourglass: Lives of the Predators* and vocabulary.com.

Zwitterion
"Is poetry anything other than craft practice & therapy?" is from poet Alice White during a conversation with Flower Conroy.

Acknowledgements

Poems have appeared (sometimes in various incarnations) in the following:

American Poetry Review: "Holy Fool," "Maggot"
Birmingham Poetry Review: "Platypus," "Sestina," "Venus (in Furs)," "Vulture," "Zonkey"
Denver Quarterly: "Zwitterion"
The Fiddlehead: "6EQUJ5"
The Florida Review: "Quagga," "Carrion"
Ghost City Press: "Deer(est)"
hex literary: "Axolotl," "Mushroom"
Inverted Syntax: "Bloodhound," "Diamondback," "Fog"
Jet Fuel Review: "Nudibranchs"
Menacing Hedge: "Snail"
Notre Dame Review: "Horseshoe Crab"
The Paris-American: "Drone"
Pedestal Magazine: "Kkaahkkaarowch"
Poem-a-Day, Academy of American Poets: "Frog"
The Poets Corner "Poetry in Motion" Collaboration: "Turtle"
Qu: "Echidna"
Sugar House Review: "Velvet"
Superstition Review: "Rabbit," "Onanism"
Tupelo Quarterly: "Parroting," "Undertaker," "Lobotomy," "Yet(i)," "Yak"
Waxwing: "Armadillo," "Machine Deep Learning (Cento)"
Whale Road Review: "Jackal"

Foremost, I'd like to thank everyone at the *Tampa Review*—especially Yuly Restrepo Garcés, Paul Corrigan, Jodi Johnson, Jay Aja, and Julie Nelson. Thank you for believing in this work.

I'd like to acknowledge the writing conferences and/or organizations which have supported my writing: the National Endowment for the Arts, MacDowell, Bread Loaf Writers' Conference, La Romita School of Art, Sewanee Writer's Conference, Tin House Writers' Conference, Community of Writers, Napa

Writer's Conference, Key West Literary Seminar, Winter Poetry and Prose Getaway, Key West Poetry Guild, and Anne McKee Artist Fund.

I've been very fortunate to have worked with and learned from many incredible mentors, including: Kim Addonizio, Kazim Ali, Renee Ashley, Rick Barot, Catherine Barnett, Gabrielle Calvocoressi, Lance Cleland, Michael Collier, Billy Collins, Natalie Diaz, Risa Denenberg, Cat Doty, Stephen Dunn, Vievee Francis, Daisy Fried, Forest Gander, Kathleen Graber, Linda Gregerson, Jennifer Grotz, Kelly Boyker Guillemette, Kenneth Hart, Bob Hass, Brenda Hillman, Edward Hirsch, Sally Keith, Keetje Kuipers, Katharyn Howd Machan, Laura McCullough, Mary Meriam, Tomás Q. Morín, Peter E. Murphy, Matthew Olzmann, Gregory Pardlo, Carl Philips, David Rivard, Mary Ruefle, Mary Jo Salter, Brenda Shaughnessy, Evie Shockley, Tom Sleigh, A.E. Stallings, Mark Strand, Diane Seuss, Mary Szybist, Angela Narciso Torres, Adam Vines, BJ Ward, Richard Weems, Mark Wunderlick, and Kevin Young.

I am grateful to have the love and support of my coven, including: Elizabeth I'm With the Band Agnes, Lisa Ampleman, Stacey Jackalope Balkun, Augustine Blaisdell, Heather Lang Cassera, Belo Miguel Cipriani, Kalo Clark, Noreen Cargill, Lisa the Summersault Fey Coutley, Alice Elliott Dark, Carly Marie DeMento, Ellen I-get-knocked-down-but-I-get-up-again Devin, Lisa The Tree Flynn, Amber Gilewski, Christine Gosnay, Court Big Dill Harler, Tracey Wasn't Me Scopa Knapp, Julia Kolchinsky, The La Romitans, Jason Lamb, Susan Landgraf, Timothy The Moth Lindner, Dawn The Gift Manning, Scott the IT Guru Manning, Donna Noodle Spruijt-Metz, Steve Oka, Risa Pappas, Patty Patten, David Pischke, Jeremy Proehl, Alessandro Quargnali-Linsley, Annie Reid, Brad Richard, Leila Rupp, James You Can't Be Rocky Russel, Phil Saint Denis Sanchez, Emily Schulten, Heidi Seaborn, Laura Francis-Sharma, Betsey Marks-Smith, Lauren Stella, Scott Stubbs, Adrian M.S. Sylva, Verta Taylor, Alice White, Ross White, Arida Davis Wright, and Edmund Zimmerman.

About the Author

LGBTQIA+ artist, former Key West Poet Laureate, and NEA and MacDowell Fellow, Flower Conroy is the author of *Snake Breaking Medusa Disorder* (NFSPS's Barbara Stevens' contest winner), *A Sentimental Hairpin*, *Greenest Grass* (Lynx's House Press' Blue Lynx Prize winner), and "And Scuttle My Balloon," co-authored with Donna Spruijt-Metz; as well as several chapbooks. Conroy has led workshops at *The Studios of Key West, La Romita School of Art, Write Here, Write Now,* and elsewhere. In addition to care-giving and freelance editing, Conroy is working on a series of *Ephemeral Altars*—impermanent assemblage art pieces that visually evoke and celebrate poetry collections. Find this series and more on Conroy's social media.

About the Book

Zoodikers: A Bestiary is set in Garamond Premier Pro digital fonts, based on original metal types by Claude Garamond and Robert Granjon that were designed and cast in Paris, France, in the sixteenth century. Also included are the Stern Pro digital font created in the twenty-first century by Jim Rimmer, Colin Kahn, and Patrick Griffin; as well as the Cormorant Garamond digital fonts designed by Christian Thalmann as inspired by the sixteenth century types of Claude Garamond. The cover features artwork by Colin and Kristine Poole. This book was designed and typeset by Jay Aja at the University of Tampa Press.

www.ingramcontent.com/pod-product-compliance
Lightning Source LLC
Chambersburg PA
CBHW060538080526
44586CB00012B/789